PUSH PURSUE PROSPER

THE WORKBOOK

Cover by: Sharon Lewis-Ruff, The Planner Consulting
Editing by: Sharon Lewis-Ruff
Formatting by: Wisdom by 30 Literary Group

ISBN: 979-8-9942619-3-4
ISBN Digital: 979-8-9942619-3-4

ABOUT THE AUTHOR

Apostle Sheila O'Brien is an Apostolic leader, prophetic voice, and transformational coach committed to equipping women to live boldly, pursue purpose, and prosper in every area of life. She serves as Co-Pastor of The Father's Heart Christian Center alongside her husband, Apostle Clive O'Brien, where she carries a mandate to restore spiritual alignment, activate spiritual authority, and turn the hearts of God's people back to Him.

With more than two decades of ministry experience, she has ministered throughout the United States and the Caribbean, teaching on deliverance, spiritual warfare, reconciliation, leadership, and the ministry of helps. She is a certified Life Coach, International Chaplain, Founder of Sheila O'Brien Ministries, 3P Coaching, and 3P Notary.

After retiring from a 32-year career with the Broward County Sheriff's Office, she shifted into full-time ministry and entrepreneurship—carrying the Kingdom blueprint: Push. Pursue. Prosper. Her ministry trains women to break cycles, conquer limiting beliefs, and walk boldly in their God-given assignment.

She is married to Apostle Clive O'Brien, and together they have one daughter.

From Tears to Triumph

Like waves that reshape the shore, these 8 weeks will gently transform you.

> *What if your silent tears could become your greatest testimony?*

Before We Begin...

This workbook is your companion for the next 8 weeks. It's not just pages to fill, it's a sacred space where your silent tears become your greatest testimony. Be honest. Be messy. Be real. This is where your breakthrough begins.

Your Commitment

I commit to showing up fully for myself during these 8 weeks. I commit to honesty, even when it's hard. I commit to doing the work, trusting the process, and believing that transformation is possible for me.

_____   _____

Who Are You Today?

In 8 weeks, you'll look back on this moment. *Capture* who you are right now, your hopes, your fears, your heart.

_____

_____

_____

_____

_____

_____

_____

_____

_____

Breaking the Silence

From Hidden Pain to Honest Expression

Rate Your Emotional Honesty

_____/_____/_____

WRITE YOUR FEELING	1			5			10
....	○	○	○	○	○	○	○
....	○	○	○	○	○	○	○
....	○	○	○	○	○	○	○
....	○	○	○	○	○	○	○
....	○	○	○	○	○	○	○

Why Do You Feel This Way?

_____

_____

_____

_____

_____

PUSH. PURSUE. PROSPER.

Rate Your Emotional Honesty

_____ / _____ / _____

WRITE YOUR FEELING	1			5			10
....	◯	◯	◯	◯	◯	◯	◯
....	◯	◯	◯	◯	◯	◯	◯
....	◯	◯	◯	◯	◯	◯	◯
....	◯	◯	◯	◯	◯	◯	◯
....	◯	◯	◯	◯	◯	◯	◯

Why Do You Feel This Way?

_____

_____

_____

_____

_____

The Silence Inventory

List 3 areas where you've been hiding your struggle.

___/___/___

I've been hiding in:

_____

_____

_____

_____

_____

I've been hiding in:

_____

_____

_____

_____

_____

Truth-Telling Practice
Write a letter you'll never send, expressing what you haven't said.

___/___/___

Truth-Telling Practice

What would change if you stopped pretending everything is fine?

___ / ___ / ___

_____

_____

_____

_____

_____

_____

_____

_____

_____

_____

Truth-Telling Practice
Who in your life deserves to see the "real" you?

_____ / _____ / _____

_____

_____

_____

_____

_____

_____

_____

_____

_____

_____

_____

_____

_____

_____

_____

_____

_____

_____

_____

_____

_____

PRAYER SPACE

Where did you feel resistance, and what does that tell you?

_____

_____

_____

_____

_____

_____

_____

_____

_____

Pressuring Through Resistance

Understanding What's Really Holding You Back

Obstacle Audit
Name your top 5 barriers. (internal and external)

_____/_____/_____

_____

_____

_____

_____

_____

Rate each fear by intensity and identify its root.

FEAR INVENTORY	1			5			10
....	○	○	○	○	○	○	○
....	○	○	○	○	○	○	○
....	○	○	○	○	○	○	○
....	○	○	○	○	○	○	○
....	○	○	○	○	○	○	○

Pinpoint the Real Issue | Not Just the Symptom

_____

_____

_____

Understand the Pattern | When Did This Start?

_____

_____

_____

Step into Small Action | What's One Mirco-Move?

_____

_____

_____

Hold Onto Hope | What's the Promise You're Believing?

_____

_____

_____

Victory Is Yours.

Document every small win, no matter how tiny.

VICTORY #1

VICTORY #2

VICTORY #3

VICTORY #4

Victory Is Yours.

Document every small win, no matter how tiny.

VICTORY #5

VICTORY #6

VICTORY #7

VICTORY #8

What obstacle surprised you when you named it?

_____

_____

_____

_____

_____

_____

_____

_____

_____

What's one pattern you're ready to break?

_____

_____

_____

_____

_____

_____

_____

_____

_____

Getting Still in the Chaos

Finding Peace When Everything Feels Urgent

List everything competing for your attention.

_____

_____

_____

_____

_____

Get Still | Seven Different 5-Minute Practices to Try

Breath Prayer   Journaling in Silence

Nature Observation   Listen to Prayer

Silent Gratitude

Body Scan

Design your personal stillness routine.

Journal what you *hear* while being still.

Which stillness practice felt most natural?

_____

_____

_____

_____

_____

_____

_____

_____

_____

What is God whispering to you in the quiet?

_____

_____

_____

_____

_____

_____

_____

_____

_____

Releasing What You're Carrying

Letting Go of Past Wounds & Future Worries

The Burden Inventory | List Everything You're Tired of Carrying

_____

_____

_____

_____

_____

Daily Surrender Statement
"Today I Release..."

_____

_____

_____

_____

_____

Gratitude Check: What freedom have you gained?

What felt lighter after you named it?

What's still hard to let go, and why?

_____

_____

_____

_____

_____

_____

_____

_____

_____

Reclaiming Your Dreams

From "Maybe Someday" to "What If Now?"

THE PERMISSION SLIP

Write yourself permission to want what you want.

Dream Excavation: If nothing could stop me, I would...

Define Your Dream Clearly

_____

_____

_____

_____

_____

Why Does this Dream Matter

_____

_____

_____

_____

Write down 3 micro-steps that you can take.

_____

_____

_____

_____

_____

What type of Support will you need to fulfill this dream?

_____

_____

_____

_____

_____

What's the worst that could happen if you don't move towards your dream?

_____

_____

_____

_____

_____

_____

CELEBRATION STRATEGY
How will you celebrate once the dream is in motion?

_____

_____

_____

_____

_____

_____

_____

_____

_____

_____

What dream surprised you when you said it out loud?

_____

_____

_____

_____

_____

_____

_____

_____

_____

What's your first small step, and when will you take it?

_____

_____

_____

_____

_____

_____

_____

_____

_____

Trusting the Process

Faith When You Can't See the Finish Line

Rate your current trust level in different areas.

TRUST INVENTORY	1			5			10
God	○	○	○	○	○	○	○
Yourself	○	○	○	○	○	○	○
Others	○	○	○	○	○	○	○
Processes	○	○	○	○	○	○	○
	○	○	○	○	○	○	○

List your Trust Barriers and why.

_____

_____

_____

_____

_____

_____

PUSH. PURSUE. PROSPER.

Collect the Evidence

Write down all of the times that God has come through for you.

VICTORY #1

VICTORY #2

VICTORY #3

VICTORY #4

PUSH. PURSUE. PROSPER.

Collect the Evidence

Write down all of the times that God has come through for you.

VICTORY #5

VICTORY #6

VICTORY #7

VICTORY #8

The Waiting Room

Write down what you can do while you're waiting for God.

The Surrender Practice
"Even though I can't see it, I believe..."

_____

_____

_____

_____

_____

_____

_____

_____

_____

Hope Anchors
Write 7 scriptures to return to when trust feels hard.

_____

_____

_____

_____

_____

_____

_____

_____

PUSH. PURSUE. PROSPER.

Where is trust hardest for you right now?

_____

_____

_____

_____

_____

_____

_____

_____

_____

What's one truth you're choosing to believe even when you can't see it?

_____

_____

_____

_____

_____

_____

_____

_____

Redefining Success

Abundance Beyond Material Gain

Planning: Set one goal in each area that feels weak.

_____

_____

_____

_____

Gratitude: Daily Practice of naming 3 things you're already prospering in.

_____

_____

_____

_____

Generosity: How will you overflow into others' lives?

_____

_____

_____

_____

Rewrite the Script
Challenge the lies you've believed about worthiness and abundance.

_____

_____

_____

_____

_____

_____

_____

_____

_____

Which area of prosperity surprised you most?

_____

_____

_____

_____

_____

_____

_____

_____

What's one shift you're committing to this week?

_____

_____

_____

_____

_____

_____

_____

_____

_____

Living in Triumph

Sustaining Transformation & Celebrating Your Breakthrough

Reflection: Who were you 8 weeks ago? Who are you now?

_____

_____

_____

_____

_____

Your New Normal: Define what consistent thriving looks like.

_____

_____

_____

_____

_____

The Ripple Effect: Who will you help with what you've learned?

_____

_____

_____

_____

_____

Identify triggers and create response plans.

_____

_____

_____

_____

90-Day Vision: Where do you want to be 3 months from now?

_____

_____

_____

_____

_____

_____

_____

_____

_____

What's your biggest win from these 8 weeks?

_____

_____

_____

_____

_____

_____

_____

_____

_____

What practice will you absolutely not abandon?

_____

_____

_____

_____

_____

_____

_____

_____

_____

Activate your authority.

Sheila O'Brien

www.sheilaobrienministries.com